uman

The Essays

First published in Italy
in 2010 by
Skira Editore S.p.A.
Palazzo Casati Stampa
via Torino 61
20123 Milano
Italy
www.skira.net

Printed and bound in Italy.
First edition

ISBN: 978-88-572-0781-0

Distributed in North America
by Rizzoli International Publications,
Inc., 300 Park Avenue South,
New York, NY 10010, USA.
Distributed elsewhere in the world
by Thames and Hudson Ltd.,
181A High Holborn, London WC1V 7QX,
United Kingdom.

Markus Ebner

Telemark

SKIRA

U

Some of the most interesting questions concerning the origin of a man's wardrobe are whether it is based on fashion and tradition, or whether it is built on pure functionality. And whether it was inherited, made-to-measure, or purchased in boutiques and specialty stores all over the world. After all, what a man wears says a lot about him – first impressions always count. Even if we deeply believe in not judging a book by its cover, the old adage holds true: you only have once chance to make a good first impression.

We often speak about fashion when we mean classic tailoring or consider military details like an epaulette, which gives the rank of an officer, as fashion statements. **Even a puffer jacket, which is used by ski aficionados to keep warm, has become a classic staple in a modern**

gentleman's wardrobe in 2010.
Worn over a well-cut suit, the puffer
vest can also make an impressive urban
statement. It is even better when the
puffer jacket is sleeveless and in
a contrasting colour to the suit, like the
Belgian designer, Veronique Branquinho,
proposed in one of her runway outings at
the Automobile Club at the Place de la
Concorde in Paris a few years back.
Or when the designer Thom Browne (who
gave boxy America back its neatly tailored
silhouette from the 1950s) designs
a range of winter wear that fits as well as
a suit wardrobe for Moncler Gamme Bleu,
going as far as creating a down-filled navy
blazer.
Clearly, these designers are breaking all
the rules and are mixing up performance
sports wear like a thermal down jacket,
designed solely to keep warm, with their
tailored silhouettes to get a new look.
The collision of fashion, sports

and tailoring is the future men's wear now. So can the classic sport of Telemark skiing be the premise for the shape of a new men's jacket? Can it be a new look for men all over the world who have never even been on the slopes of an Alpine resort? The answer is yes and we give this trend an emphatic thumbs-up. Credible inspirations like classic sport or military uniforms are the basis of newness in men's design. Let's face it: **the future of successful fashion businesses will be in providing the one piece of clothing a customer does not have in his closet yet, and which has a real intrinsic sense of value.** So this essay explores the possibilities of what this means for men's fashion and takes a close look at the different kinds of inspirations and foundations a jacket style can have. I'd also like to shine a spotlight on **the deeply Mittel-European Austrian capital Vienna and some of the past and present players there. Some of them were pioneers in creating new silhouettes and looks in menswear that still dominate the current scene.**

Let's begin with Helmut Lang, a fashion designer from Vienna, one of the innovators who stood at the forefront of fusing utilitarian elements with classic tailoring. It is a little-known fact that Vienna is one of the three capitals of custom-made men's design and tailoring. Everybody has heard of London's Savile Row or Neapolitan suit making, but few are in the know about Vienna's rigorous cuts. Maybe the city's tourism board needs a better marketing department because the city is steeped in old traditions. Here, old world charm is naturally brought into the now by young family hands who are willing to uphold the rigorous craftsmanship and play with new design. Where else can you find an Adolf-Loos-designed haberdasher like Knize? Or a boot-maker like Markus Scheer working in the seventh generation of his family business? And in what other city does the annual Opera Ball make an entire city waltz and shine in elaborate tuxedos and tails, bringing magnificent business to the local tailors and dry cleaners?

Knize has been at the forefront of bringing a streamlined silhouette to Vienna's upper crust and wealthy clients from Eastern Europe. **And it comes as no surprise that Vienna is the new men's wear Mecca** when you realize that three recent professors at the local fashion school, the University of Applied Arts in Vienna, were Helmut Lang, Raf Simons, and Veronique Branquinho.

The Austrian and Belgian designers have been the dominant influences in men's clothes. Lang's "hand" can be seen from the mid-1990s to his last collection in 2003 and Simons and Branquinho have exerted their influence since then; their shared focus has been the cut and function of a garment, nothing more, and nothing less. Now, a fresh wave of graduates of their fashion design programme seeks the spotlight with fashion shows in Paris.

The names to remember include Petar Petrov and Ute Ploier, designers who love the cult of tailoring but update it with codes of the street. Originally from Sofia, Bulgaria, Petar Petrov is a talent to watch, as he likes to walk in Helmut Lang's footsteps.

By playing with military elements with an Eastern-European twist, Austria seems a natural launching pad for designers hailing from the East due to its proximity to the borders of Hungary, Slovakia and Slovenia.

Lang always brought his students to the workrooms at Knize, so they would understand fundamentally the construction of a garment before they applied their fashion fantasies to a sketchpad. So Lang could hardly escape the influence of the straight lines favoured by Knize. He has made it his signature to combine elements of army clothing like light reflecting stripes with his tailored coats. One of his obsessions was the elongation of a classic silhouette by letting cords and strings dangle from the body. It stems from an original fishtail army parka, which was used during the Korean War where the parka was standard issue for the US troops shipping off to less than friendly conditions in the Far East. Soldiers tied the strings together to keep their legs warm, but for Lang the dangling strings became a fashion statement and over time a new look developed which was the urban uniform of the 1990s: **utilitarian clothing with elegance. It was the freedom of the fashion designer to combine unrelated elements like army clothing with classic tailoring that made the new look.**

And as for Raf Simons: he is a trained industrial designer and has been bringing a distinctly different eye to the approach of crafting a garment. He goes as far as using ceramics by the Belgian artist Pol Chambost as an inspiration for a collection and its silhouette. Simons is more often inspired by extreme volumes and is looking to move fashion forward by doing so. Where else can you find a nipped waist women's silhouette in a men's collection? This is a good approach to come up with newness and innovation.

Rudolf Niedersüß, Knize's owner and master tailor, has a different approach when he works on a jacket for a client. Let's say he has to do work for an avid shooter and hunter. Here the client's needs and wishes govern the entire design process. Niedersüß now has to think about making a jacket with a generous range of motion in the shoulder area so the shooter can raise his rifle quickly; at the same time the design cannot use extra fabric because the jacket needs to retain its elegance and straight lines. Niedersüß only has to think about the functionality of the garment and has to channel his skills to get the result the client desires. Hence, an intricate pattern of folds and pleats under the shoulder is developed to create a look based on tailoring necessities. A deep pleat in the back of the jacket to improve the range of motion and a half belt around the back to support the shooter are anchors of the look.

Not that this idea is unique to Austria. In Britain, this sort of tailoring trick of using a half belt at the back is named a Norfolk Jacket, after the county in which the Prince of Wales, later Edward VII, spent so much time hunting with his friends in the late nineteenth century. Designed as a shooting coat that did not block the elbow when it is raised to fire, the Norfolk Jacket was worn by all of Edward's party when they came to hunt at the royal residence of Sandringham House in Norfolk. The Royal Family still spends each New Year at Sandringham,

1 *Frank E. Schoonover's*
The Cross Country Skiers,
oil on canvas, 1939

2 *Telemark is the style of fluid
curves with "free-heel" skis.
Begun in Norway in the late
nineteenth century, when Sondre
Norheim took part in a ski
jumping competition*

3 Illustrierte Sportzeitung, *1926.
Telemark is shown as a "dance
on skis"*

4 *An early technique was to use a long wooden iron-tipped stick to direct the skiers' turns*

5 *Rivella models on show at the 1956 Winter Olympics in Cortina*

located close to the shores of the North Sea, and the Norfolk half belt is still featured in all hunting attire. Edward VII was so obsessed with hunting that he ordered all clocks on the state to be set half an hour ahead of GMT, so he and his friends would have more time for hunting – and wearing their Norfolk Jackets.

The deeply Mittel-European culture of catering to a client's needs or the savvy way of mixing military and sports elements is at the forefront of what's new and important again. So let's apply these thoughts to the look of a new jacket for the men of the slopes.

Let's travel to the region of Telemark in the southern parts of Norway.

Telemark is a term for skiing that uses the **Telemark turn, which is also known as "free heel skiing". Unlike Alpine skiing equipment, the skis used for Telemark have a binding that only connects the boot to the ski at the toes, just as in cross-country skiing.** Hence, this is not necessarily a sport with lots of pace and speed, where streamlined and aerodynamic clothes are needed. **It sounds more like a gentlemanly and leisurely sport, not one to compete in but more relax and enjoy.** And it is a sport where the skier takes his time and doesn't break out in major sweats. When he sees a beautiful vista, he might just stop and take it in. Even better, he might pull out a flask from his jacket and have himself a wee shot of hot rum with honey, or a special Islay single malt to stay warm and happy. Of course, his Telemark jacket has a pocket that is just big enough for a sterling silver flask. From Christofle, for example.

The Telemark turn came to the attention of the Norwegian public in 1868, when Sondre Norheim took part in a ski jumping competition. Norheim's technique of fluid turns soon dominated skiing, and in Norway it continued to do so well into the next century. As the sport is deeply rooted in history, the design should reflect this as well. Maybe its colour scheme could even be based on the Norwegian flag with bold use of red and blue. Needless to say, all the pockets should be equipped with buttons closed on hand-sewn buttonholes, not Velcro or other high-tech material closures.

The revival of the Telemark technique, after its decline from popularity in the mid-

1940s, started in United States in the 1970s. Telemark skiing was a back-to-basics reaction to the high-tech equipment developments of Alpine skiing, and the increasing reliance on crowded groomed pistes served by ever larger and faster mechanical ski lifts. **So Telemark is a clear response to a high-tech and sporty style where functional, water repellent fabrics that can breathe are of utmost importance.** This is not a Gore-Tex moment. Rather, it calls more for something like a mix of thick cashmere, albeit with technical finishes, so the natural fibre is modernized with elegance. Clearly, the Telemark skier is not someone who worries about maximum performance when it comes to his clothing; more importantly, what he cares about is maximum enjoyment. In fact, the après-ski moment might be just as important to the sportsman. So we should think of pockets to store his sunglasses, or else a classic pocket to put a handkerchief or a flower when taking a glass of ice-cold champagne or hot rum with coffee. **In general, the foundation would be a classic style like a sophisticated sports coat.**

Could it be that the era of fast fashion might just be coming to an end? The time when the demands of department store buyers, and their obsession with placing logos on anything in a man's wardrobe drove the industry, might be eclipsed? Typical of this new direction – at least on the other side of the Atlantic – is a nostalgic mood that is wafting through men's style and clothing in New York. A longing for a certain sort of gentlemanly, literary past, where men drank bourbon, read Walt Whitman, and happily wore styles of clothes like their grandfathers had worn before them, albeit with more finishes and fabrics.

Thom Browne announced that his key new idea for spring 2010 was the "Robinson Crusoe suit": a distressed Prince of Wales linen number, with obvious repairs. Robert Geller, voted the Best New Menswear Designer in America by *GQ* magazine, said he was inspired by 1950s vacations on Germany's Baltic seaside, while British designer Simon Spurr modelled his crisp gents' looks on vintage Helmut Newton photos. **Nostalgia was also apparent in the emergence of a new class of Downtown Gent spotted throughout lower Manhattan.** Their look – miniature bow ties, worn Harris tweed jackets, plaid shirts, pre-teen pants to expose sock-free feet and two-tone brogues. Their restaurant of choice, Freemans, is a "rugged clandestine, colonial American tavern" on the Bowery that recalls the literary tables of 1930s Manhattan, when men were scholarly, drank their whiskey neat, and Blackberry was a pie. It this world twitter is not a revolutionary new means of communication but superficial ramblings for twits. **Like too fast fashion, overly fashion talk is the enemy of the sophisticated gentleman; the composed individual who takes time to get things exactly right.**

It's all about a longing for poise. Accomplished Telemark skiers, like accomplished Alpine skiers, for instance, keep their torsos vertical and oriented downhill while linking turns, thus avoiding turning too far. This position also allows greater control over the fine-tuning of weight distribution. Hence,

it will be important to give the jacket wearer maximum range of motion in the shoulder area. Similar to the hunting man's jacket offered by master tailor Rudolf Niedersüß at Knize, we foresee a construction that provides an additional amount of fabric that allows for sudden movements of the arms and the torso. And one more thought to the fabric: a clever fabric mix might not be too new-school and a bit of nylon could possibly be mixed up with cashmere and would allow for the desired effect of a fabric being stretched easily.

Surely we are entering a new era of rugged individualism, where the polar scientist is the new romantic explorer. Here I am writing this essay as the world prepares for the Copenhagen climate summit and the media is saturated with imagery of Antarctic researchers dashing across bays in Zodiacs to obtain core samples of disappearing glaciers and analyse snow density in clothing that neatly encapsulates both technological innovation and common sense.

The combination of bitter cold and strong winds in the Antarctic can cause a person to become frostbitten or hypothermic. But modern cold-weather gear is light years away from the gear available to the original Antarctic explorers, like Carsten Borchgrevink, the first man to winter on Antarctica in 1900, or Ernest Shackleton, who in January 1909 made a southern march that established a record Farthest South latitude from the South Pole. These heroes had to make do with heavy layers of itchy woollen fabrics and outer layers that would soak up the moisture produced by sweat. Today, down – the fine, insulating

underfeathers of waterbirds – provides
clothes with lightweight warmth. Yet
the real insulation is provided by the
air trapped in down's fine structure.
That means down clothing can provide
inches of insulation without adding too
much weight, and though down does not
provide good insulation when it gets wet,
that should not be a problem since it
hasn't rained in millions of years at the
South Pole.

This clothing, whose practicality, finish
and look has morphed into men's wear
globally, is the very antithesis of fast
fashion. It recognizes the wisdom of the
past while at the same time incorporating
the advances of modern science to
create a style that is hyper-functional
yet rooted in the gentleman heroes of a
more gracious era. They were men who
took risks, who were not afraid to fail,
and often paid the ultimate price for

their bravery. Shackleton died of a heart attack at the age of 47, while his ship, the *Quest*, was moored in South Georgia en route to attempt the greatest Antarctic journey: crossing the continent from sea to sea via the pole.

Let's not forget that falling on your face is also part of the fun of skiing. In order to protect our Telemark gentleman, we suggest the inclusion of a hoodie in the jacket, not one that rolls into a lumpy sausage in a men's neck but a real nice protection piece on the outside. Maybe it can have a zipped-up fur lining inside, which can be taken out after a particularly wet fall.

Contrary to popular opinion, men of a ripe old age do continue to ski, which is good news in an era when medical science grants us remarkable and lengthening longevity. Just like another great Norwegian, Stein Eriksen, the first individual outside of the Alps to win an Olympic men's Alpine ski medal. Though he celebrated his eightieth birthday two years ago, Stein still skies daily around his home in Deer Valley, Utah.

One last thing: poles for Telemark skiers are optional. With or without poles, the skier's hands should be in front of their body. Some Telemark skiers continue to ski with a single long pole or "lurk" held in both hands in traditional style. The lurk should only contact the snow on the inside of the turn, though some find better balance results if it contacts the snow on the outside of the turn. But, needless to say, this lurk is a fantastic eye catcher when gliding into the après-ski bar area. The pole is an expression of supreme individuality and we foresee coordinating colours with our jacket, which means the pole needs to be a solid red or blue to go with the piping on the sleeves of our cashmere-nylon Telemark style jacket.

In sum, the definition of a true gentleman's wardrobe is where fashion and functionality meet in a happy confluence of style.

François Berthoud
Born in Switzerland,
1961, lives and works in
Zurich. He is known for
his fashion illustrations.
Since the mid-1980s,
François Berthoud has
been mainly engaged
in artistic activities.
His high-impact images
bring art, fashion
and communication
together. He has
published books, staged
exhibitions and realized
special fashion projects.
He is a contributor
to major magazines
worldwide.

Markus Ebner is the
founder of Achtung,
Germany's directional
fashion magazine
(www.achtung-mode.
com) and Sepp (www.
sepp-magazine.com),
a unique publication
that brings together
football and fashion.
He is the men's fashion
critic for Frankfurter
Allgemeine Zeitung and
is currently dreaming of
a jacket that will keep
him warm and make
him look ultra-chic at
the World Cup 2010 in
South Africa.

The publisher would like to thank the
following for the use of their photographs
in this publication, pp. 14–15:
1. © American Illustrators Gallery, NYC /
www.sapworldwide.com / The Bridgeman Art
Library / Archivi Alinari
5. Archivio Toscani / Gestione Archivi Alinari,
Florence

**cover and back cover image
by François Berthoud**